Tableaus of Tbilisi

FROM RUSTAVELI AVENUE TO NARIKALA FORTRESS

A TRAVEL PHOTO ART BOOK

LAINE CUNNINGHAM

Tableaus of Tbilisi

From Rustaveli Avenue to Narikala Fortress

A Travel Photo Art Book

Published by Sun Dogs Creations
Changing the World One Book at a Time
Print ISBN: 978-1-946732-90-3

Cover Design by Angel Leya

Copyright © 2019 Laine Cunningham

All rights reserved. No part of this book may be reproduced in any form or by any means, electronic, mechanical, digital, photocopying or recording, except for the inclusion in a review, without permission in writing from the publisher.

THE TRAVEL PHOTO ART SERIES

Bikes of Berlin

Necropolises of New Orleans I & II

Ruins of Rome I & II

Ancients of Assisi I & II

Panoramas of Portugal

Nuances of New York

Glimpses of Germany

Impressions of Italy

Altitudes of the Alps

Knights Through the Ages

Coast of California

Utopia of the Unicorn

Flourishes of France

Portraits of Paris

Grandeur in the Republic of Georgia

SQUARE ROOT

WANDERESS

ROOK ROCK

OLD TOWN AFTERNOON

DELPHINIUM

FACELIFT

ART OF THE AGES

NYAN LIVE

STEP BEYOND

MADCAP

RIVEN

IGLOOS

CHERRY TREES

AGING GRANDEUR

SOLO SNOOZLE

THREE TREES

PASTA

FLAGS

FUNDAMENTAL

INFORMATION DESK

SQUEEZE

UNDULATE

ACCESS

SILO

KARTLIS DEDA

About the Author

Laine Cunningham's books take readers around the world. *The Family Made of Dust* is set in the Australian Outback, while *Reparation* is a novel of the American Great Plains. Her women's travel adventure memoir *Woman Alone: A Six-Month Journey Through the Australian Outback* appeals to fans of *Wild* and *Eat Pray Love*.

Fiction

The Family Made of Dust

Beloved

Reparation

Nonfiction

Woman Alone

On the Wallaby Track: Australian Words and Phrases

Seven Sisters: Messages from Aboriginal Australia

Writing While Female or Black or Gay

The Zen of Travel
The Zen of Gardening
Zen in the Stable
The Zen of Chocolate
The Zen of Dogs

The Wisdom of Puppies
The Wisdom of Babies
The Wisdom of Weddings

Bikes of Berlin
Necropolises of New Orleans I & II
Ruins of Rome I & II
Ancients of Assisi I & II
Panoramas of Portugal
Nuances of New York
Glimpses of Germany
Impressions of Italy
Altitudes of the Alps
Knights Through the Ages
Coast of California
Utopia of the Unicorn
Flourishes of France
Portraits of Paris
Tableaus of Tbilisi
Grandeur in the Republic of Georgia

www.ingramcontent.com/pod-product-compliance
Lightning Source LLC
Chambersburg PA
CBHW041321110526
44591CB00021B/2867